Pro Wrestling's Black World Champions

Pro Wrestling's Black World Champions

Julian L.D. Shabazz
and David L. Shabazz

Awesome Records
Clinton, South Carolina

Books by Julian L.D. Shabazz

Black Stars of Professional Wrestling (3rd Edition)

It's Time For Some Action!

How to Be a Player in the Publishing Industry

Roar of the Tigers!
(An Illustrated History of Benedict College Athletics 1907-2005)

How to Be a Player (14 Principles for Success in the Game of Life)

Dolemite - The Story of Rudy Ray Moore
(with David L. Shabazz)

The Assassination of Black Radio

The United States vs. Hip-Hop

Pro Wrestling's Black World Champions

Julian L.D. Shabazz
and David L. Shabazz

Pro Wrestling's Black World Champions

Copyright © 2022 by Julian L. D. Shabazz and David L. Shabazz

Second Edition -- First Printing

All Rights Reserved
Published in the United States by Awesome Records

No part of this book may be reproduced or utilized in any form by any means, electronic or mechanical, including photocopying, recording or by any information storage and retrieval system, without permission in writing from the publisher.

Library of Congress Control Number: 2022913299

ISBN: 978-1893680-16-6

Manufactured in the United States of America

For the unsung Black wrestlers who paved the way

Preface

It gives me great pleasure to update this book on the Black professional wrestlers who are recognized as world championship title holders. Many more Black professional wrestlers have an opportunity to not only challenge for the world title, but to also enjoy a title reign. In the past, many wrestling promoters erroneously assumed that Black wrestlers were not "over" with the audiences. First, that totally ignores the rabid fan base of Black supporters in particular but also other non-white fans who make up the total audience. While wrestling's predominant audience is white, the next false assumption is that white audiences would not accept a black world heavyweight champion. Everyone has their personal likes and dislikes, but wrestling fans know that promoters have thoroughly tested an individual for their toughness, ability to fight (in case a real world situation calls for it), personality and charisma before bestowing them with the honor of being called "world heavyweight champion."

My brother, Julian L. D. Shabazz, wrote the first edition as an eBook in 2009 - ten years after the publication of his groundbreaking title *Black Stars of Professional Wrestling*. The small booklet was a mostly a special project for Julian to groom his oldest son Rassoull- who illustrated the original cover. A lot has changed since the first edition. Over the last 13 years, there have been five more Black men to wear the world heavyweight title belt around their waist. There are more Black women winning tag team titles and division or brand titles so it appears promising that more Black women will compete for and eventually win the women's heavyweight championship.

This book highlights the Black men and women who have had an opportunity to be the champion or the face of one of the major American wrestling promotions. Before profiling each champion, the preface will briefly explore wrestling's roots in Africa, its growth in America and how several independent promotions grew to become the modern major wrestling companies.

Ancient African wrestling

The story of Black wrestlers would be incomplete without mentioning the legacy which began in Africa. Judging by the pictographs alone, wrestling was ancient Egypt's most popular sport. Artwork found in the city of Beni Hasan shows hundreds of wrestling holds and maneuvers. Depictions of the ancient Greek system implies their wrestlers focused on throws while Egyptian wrestling specialized in ground submissions. Scholars tend to highlight the Egyptian system, however, historian Thomas Desch-Obi notes that fighting sports were part of every tribal community throughout the African continent. One popular African wrestling tradition is the Senegalese art of *laamb* which has been practiced for thousands of years. It has been compared to the Greco-Roman style of wrestling. There are also other fighting styles akin to no-hold barred and catch-as-catch-can prevalent throughout the various tribes across the African continent.

Wrestling was also a popular sport in ancient Nubia. According to the article *Wrestling in Ancient Nubia* (Carroll, 1988), Nubian wrestlers appeared in at least five ancient Egyptian drawings. Combat sports such as wrestling and stick fighting were used for military training. While wrestling remained popular in Egypt, the sport thrived after the Greek conquest in 332 BC and again in 30 BC after the Roman conquest of Egypt. Wrestling eliminated much of the brutality and evolved into more of a spectator sport eventually becoming one of the first modern Olympic sports in 1896. For more information on ancient African wrestling, also read Elphinstone Dayrell's *Folk Stories from Southern Nigeria*, Chinua Achebe's novel *Things Fall Apart* and *Games of the Ancients* by Steve Craig.

Modern wrestling in the United States

In the early 1800s, wrestling was a popular frontier sport. Many of the early American presidents including George Washington and Abraham Lincoln were local wrestlers. Before the

1920's, professional wrestling was considered a legitimate sport with the same high level of esteem as boxing. Noted Russian wrestler George Hackenschmidt competed in both Greco-Roman and catch-as-catch-can (or freestyle) wrestling during the late 19th century. American wrestler Frank Gotch defeated Hackenschmidt in the early 1900s. During this time, boxing was increasingly becoming more prominent than wrestling. Upon Gotch's retirement in 1913, professional wrestling maneuvers became more extravagant and theatrical with scripted storylines pitting heroes against villains.

The National Wrestling Alliance (NWA) was formed in 1948 as both a promotion and a governing body over several wrestling promotions in different territories throughout the United States. The owners of the independent wrestling promotions made up the NWA's board of directors. The NWA was a collective that allowed promotions to exchange wrestlers among their territories, provided protection for each member promotion and the board selected one wrestler as the recognized world champion. The NWA was well organized and served as the governing body for professional wrestling in North America as NWA territories once spread across the United States and Canada. Before television became a staple in American households, wrestlers could periodically perform in a different territory for another promotion under a different name and alias. With television, professional wrestling experienced its first Golden Age from 1940s through the 1950s. Professional wrestling's popularity grew to new levels through performers like Gorgeous George, "Nature Boy" Buddy Rogers and Lou Thesz. However, the NWA's stronghold of the territories began to loosen towards the end of the 1950s.

Independent promotions re-emerge from the NWA

Verne Gagne's American Wrestling Association (AWA) based in Minneapolis, left the NWA in 1960. In January 1963, Lou Thesz defeated Buddy Rogers for the NWA World Heavyweight Championship. The Capitol Wrestling Corporation (CWC) promotion headed by Vincent J. McMahon and Joseph "Toots" Mondt, felt Thesz did not draw huge crowds like Rogers and thus refused to acknowledge Thesz as the champion. They withdrew the CWC from the NWA and formed the World Wide Wrestling Federation (WWWF) in April 1963 with Rogers as their champion. Despite leaving the NWA, McMahon remained a member of the NWA's Board of Directors. The WWWF rejoined the NWA during wrestling's decline in the 1970s. The NWA became the premier organization once again on the strength of Georgia Championship Wrestling. The promotion was the first nationally televised wrestling program on the Turner Broadcasting System (TBS) cable network. Jim Crockett who was the NWA president at the time bought Georgia Championship Wrestling and its popular Saturday night program called World Championship Wrestling. In 1988, TBS bought Georgia Championship Wrestling and renamed it World Championship Wrestling (WCW). In September 1993, the Atlanta-based WCW officially left the NWA to become an independent promotion.

In 1979, the WWWF changed its name to the World Wrestling Federation (WWF) while still a member of the NWA. The WWF left the NWA for good when Vince K. McMahon bought the company from his father in 1982. The WWF became World Wrestling Entertainment (WWE) in 2002.

On August 27, 1994, Eastern Championship Wrestling held a tournament for the vacant NWA World Heavyweight Championship. Instead of accepting the NWA title, tournament winner Shane Douglas declared himself the first ECW World Heavyweight Champion. The company withdrew from the NWA and later renamed itself Extreme Championship Wrestling.

In June 2002, Jerry Jarrett and his son Jeff formed the Nashville-based NWA: Total Nonstop Action (TNA) wrestling. TNA was not a member but had a strong relationship with the NWA. TNA (now Impact Wrestling) was allowed control over the NWA world heavyweight championship and the world tag team championship until 2007.

In 2019, another father and son team - Shahid and Tony Khan, formed All Elite Wrestling (AEW) based in Jacksonville, Florida. AEW currently produces the two-hour weekly show *Dynamite* on TBS and a one-hour weekly show *Rampage* on Turner Network

Television (TNT). AEW is currently the second largest wrestling promotion in the United States behind the WWE.

Ring of Honor (ROH) Wrestling premiered on March 21, 2009 on the HDNet until 2011. The Sinclair Broadcast Group aired ROH's weekly wrestling program until it was bought by AEW in March 2022.

This brief overview identifies the current and former major United States wrestling companies – AEW, ECW, ROH, TNA/Impact Wrestling, WCW and the WWE. The NWA is still in existence; however, it is currently not recognized as one of the major wrestling promotions. The Black professional wrestlers profiled in this book won the world title from one of these major wrestling promotions.

There is also a section paying homage to the forerunners who paved the way for modern Black wrestlers and others who won titles after a promotion lost its stature. This publication is an effort to continue my brother's years of dedication to ensure Black wrestlers received proper acknowledgement, recognition and fan support. Perhaps one day, black world champions will become so commonplace until a book like this is no longer necessary.

-David L. Shabazz
April 2022

Pro Wrestling's Black World Champions

Julian L.D. Shabazz & David L. Shabazz

Pro Wrestling's Black World Champions

Introduction

In 1999, I independently published the book *Black Stars of Professional Wrestling*. It was a labor of love and respect for the African American performers in professional wrestling. Pro wrestling has always been one of my favorite sporting events and many stars were inspirations and even heroes of mine. Little did I know at the time, I was writing a landmark book on the subject.

The book immediately took off in terms of sales and notoriety and much to my surprise, I became identified with it around the globe. Articles were written in newspapers, magazines, and the internet. I did numerous interviews on television, radio, and in various print media. The publication of that book opened many doors for me in the past ten years. One of the many opportunities that came my way was the chance to write freelance articles for various publications.

One of those was an internet-based publication called *Kayfabe Magazine*. I was contacted by Dr. Brett Gates of the magazine who allowed me to write a series of articles for the online magazine. The first article I wrote was called "Pro Wrestling's Black World Champs: A Short History." In that article, I focused on the handful of African Americans who have been placed in the top position as world heavyweight champion of a major North American wrestling promotion. This little book is a much more expanded and revised version of what I started with that article.

Consider the fact that hundreds of Black professional wrestlers have participated in the ring at least since the 1800s and only nine have ever been recognized as world champs. Even further, six of those won their titles within the last decade or so. Quite an oversight, wouldn't you say? Believe it or not, many wrestling promoters barred integrated matches until the 1960's. And for a number of years, there was something - fictitious as it was – called the "World Negro Heavyweight Title."

I realize that race is an issue that many would rather not discuss, especially in the context of sports. However, I only wish to give a little background and pay tribute to the few Black world champions in professional wrestling.

-Julian L.D. Shabazz

(2009)

FORERUNNERS

Pro Wrestling's Black World Champions

BEARCAT WRIGHT

By all accounts, the controversial Edward "Bearcat" Wright was a very good wrestler and an extremely proud man. A former boxer, Wright worked all over the world throughout his career. The tall, huge man was very popular with fans and always drew money as an attraction. At 6'6" tall, he was a good ring worker who originated and popularized many of the movements that later became stereotypical for Black wrestlers.

Even though Wright was very popular and successful as a performer, he nonetheless shared the frustrations of so many African American athletes of his day. In some areas of the United States, promoters had a ban on integrated matches and it was unheard of for a Black wrestler to be on top as a promotion's world champion. Wright repeatedly wrestled against the same Black wrestlers in town after town.

He saw the response of the fans to his popularity and finally he'd had enough of what he felt was second-class treatment of Black wrestlers. It was after yet another segregated match in Gary, Indiana in 1960 when Wright grabbed the house microphone and announced that he'd never wrestle in a segregated arena again. He was promptly suspended by the Indiana State Athletic Commission but his plea was heard by many. The NAACP came out in support of Wright and later the sport was desegregated in Indiana.

On April 4, 1961, Wright defeated Walter "Killer" Kowalski to become the first Black world heavyweight champion. The title was under the banner of the Big Time Wrestling promotion headed by Tony Santos in New England. Two years later, he captured the World Wrestling Association (WWA) version of the title when he defeated "Classy" Freddie Blassie. Wright created more controversy with that organization also by refusing to lose the title and was later stripped of the world title by the WWA.

Bearcat Wright's proud stand and often controversial nature may have given promoters headaches, but served in many ways as opening previously closed doors for Black pro wrestlers. Wright himself remained popular with fans and a trendsetter for those who followed. He passed away on August 28, 1982 at the age of 50, but his groundbreaking legacy of triumph and success lives on. Wright was inducted into the legacy wing of the WWE's Hall of Fame in 2017.

BOBO BRAZIL

Houston Harris was one of the most popular professional wrestlers of all time. Wrestling under the name Bobo Brazil, he was a real hit with fans of all races throughout his entire career. Standing 6'8" tall and weighing nearly 300 pounds, Brazil is often referred to as "the Jackie Robinson of professional wrestling" because of his immense success in crossing over and breaking down racial and ethnic barriers in the ring.

His popularity was such that he is one of the former claimants to the fictitious "World Negro Heavyweight Title." He became so popular that he was instrumental in crossing over to wrestling any of the top white stars of his day. The leading pro wrestling conglomerate of the day, the National Wrestling Alliance (NWA) allowed him to wrestle and defeat "Nature Boy" Buddy Rogers for the NWA World Heavyweight title in 1962. Although the title change was not officially recognized by the NWA, it shows how his career took on such a ground-breaking trajectory.

Brazil won a recognized world title on September 2, 1966 when he beat Buddy Austin in Los Angeles for the World Wrestling Association (WWA) world title. He actually held that belt twice, winning it again on January 12, 1968. When the WWA rejoined the NWA, there was a unification bout between Brazil and NWA champion Gene Kiniski. The match ended in a draw with Kiniski retaining the title.

Bobo Brazil's long career was filled with championships and success all over the world. In 1994, he was inducted into the World Wrestling Entertainment (WWE) Hall of Fame. Bobo Brazil died on January 20, 1998 at the age of 74, silencing a career that spanned over four decades.

CHAMPIONS FROM MAJOR FEDERATIONS

RON SIMMONS

Ronald Simmons is one of the most influential athletes in the history of professional wrestling. Simmons is the first universally recognized Black world heavyweight champion from a major wrestling promotion. He also held the world tag team title in both WCW and three times in the WWF (WWE). He also played a direct role in elevating a young Rocky Maivia into the future champion known simply as The Rock.

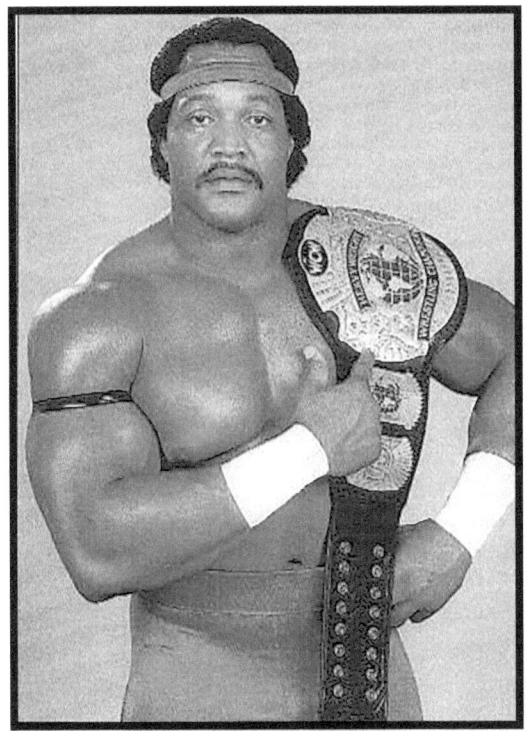

Before lacing up his wrestling boots, Simmons was a standout college football player. He was a consensus All-American nose guard at Florida State University. Playing for the legendary coach Bobby Bowden, his senior year at Florida State was so great that he finished eighth in the voting for the Heisman Trophy. After his heralded college career ended, he was drafted by the Cleveland Browns of the National Football League (NFL). He also played pro football for the Ottawa Rough Riders of the Canadian Football League (CFL) and the Tampa Bay Bandits of the United States Football League (USFL).

After retiring from professional football, Simmons began training with famed wrestling trainer Hiro Matsuda and began his career as a pro wrestler. With his physique and football credentials,

Simmons made a striking appearance and rapidly rose to the top in the NWA and World Championship Wrestling (WCW). In 1986, he joined Jim Crockett Promotions and appeared in the Great American Bash. As a rookie, Simmons scored signature wins over Ivan Koloff, The Barbarian and Rodney Anoa'i (later known as Yokozuna). He remained undefeated for over a year until he lost to Ivan Koloff.

In 1989, he teamed with Butch Reed to form the tag team

Doom. Both members originally wore masks until losing to the Steiner Brothers in February 1990. In January 1991, Doom became recognized as the first WCW World Tag Team champions. A month later, they lost the titles to the Fabulous Freebirds. Simmons returned to singles wrestling and began a quest for the world title. Ron Simmons is the first universally recognized Black world champion of a major federation. Whereas Bearcat Wright and Bobo Brazil held versions of the world title, Simmons won the WCW World

Heavyweight Championship on August 2, 1992 by defeating Big Van Vader.

Simmons held the title for several months before losing it back to Vader. He moved on to compete briefly for the original Extreme Championship Wrestling (ECW) promotion and then on to the WWF/E. On the WWF's roster, Simmons remained popular in various roles as Farooq, leader of the Nation of Domination and later forming the Acolytes Protection Agency (APA) with tag team partner Bradshaw (JBL). A less significant but immensely popular part of his legacy is the four-letter word "damn." After something goes wrong, Simmons would say damn to himself. His partner Bradshaw noticed fans in different cities would utter the phrase back to him during matches. Simmons officially debuted the catchphrase in 2007 during a segment with King Booker and John Cena.

Throughout his career, Simmons was a Triple Crown champion in WCW. He won the world heavyweight title, world tag team title and United States tag team championship. In the WWE, he held the tag team championship three times with Bradshaw. Simmons was inducted into the WWE Hall of Fame in 2012. Although Simmons faded from world title contention after his historic run as a singles wrestler, he is the blueprint for the modern black wrestling world champions.

JACQUELINE

The very athletic Jacqueline Moore is perhaps one of the most accomplished female pro wrestlers of all-time. For years in wrestling, females were primarily used as "arm pieces" and "eye candy;" especially in today's brand of "sports-entertainment." Moore, a skilled wrestler, kickboxer and martial artist, never relied on her looks or physique to capture the attention of wrestling fans. She started her career under the tutelage of General Skandor Akbar.

Being the only female in the wrestling school, Jacqueline had to train with the men.

She made her debut with World Class Championship Wrestling under the name Sweet Georgia Brown, competing in the United States and Japan. In 1991, she debuted in the United States Wrestling Association as "Miss Texas." Originally, a heel valet for Team Texas, she routinely attacked the opponents and even interfered in matches. As Miss Texas, she was the first United States Wrestling Association's (USWA) Women's Champion. She would win the title on eight occasions before coming to WCW in 1997 where she made a name for herself as a strong and athletic manager of various male wrestlers including Kevin Sullivan and Harlem Heat.

After a brief but influential stint in WCW, Jacqueline joined the World Wrestling Federation (now WWE) in 1998 as the "girlfriend" of "Marvelous" Marc Mero. This instantly set up a feud with Mero's estranged wife Sable. After months of feuding, Jaqueline eventually defeated Sable to become the first African

American WWF Women's World Champion. After a two-month reign, she lost the title to Sable. However, Jacqueline won the WWF Women's title for a second time in 2000.

During her tenure in WWF, she also participated in mixed-gender matches where she wrestled both men and women – something she trained for since the early days. In 2004, she defeated Chavo Guerrero, Jr to become the Cruiserweight champion. She lost the title in a rematch to Guerrero and was released from the company.

In November 2004, she joined Total Nonstop Action (TNA) wrestling. Jacqueline continued to wrestle women and referee men's matches before transitioning to working behind the scenes. Her last match with TNA was in 2013 – the same year she was inducted into the WWE Hall of Fame.

THE ROCK

Dwayne Douglas Johnson is not only one of the most famous pro wrestlers of all time, but also one of Hollywood's most successful actors. Johnson's movies have grossed over $10 billion worldwide making him one of the highest grossing actors. Before he was a top box office draw and businessman, he wrestled full time for eight years in the WWF/WWE. Debuting on the circuit as "Flex Kavana," he later became known as "Rocky Maivia" – as homage to his famous wrestling father "Soul Man" Rocky Johnson and grandfather, the High Chief Peter Maivia. The third generation wrestler reached superstar status as "The Rock."

As a wrestler, The Rock is a Triple Crown champion in the WWE. He is a 10 time world heavyweight champion in the World Wrestling Federation (WWF/WWE). The Rock is also a two-time Intercontinental Champion and has held the world tag team belt five times. Johnson was born in Hayward, California. He is the son of former wrestler Rocky Johnson, a Black Canadian and Samoan mother Ata Maivia. His father and partner Tony Atlas were the first Black world tag team champions in the WWF. His maternal grandmother was the first female professional wrestling promoter when she took over Polynesia Pacific Pro Wrestling after the death of her husband Peter Maivia.

Wrestling is in Johnson's blood; however, it was not the first sport where he found success. As a high school football player, he was named "player of the year" and received a full scholarship to play football at the University of Miami. At Miami, he was a member of the national championship team and as a senior was named pre-season All-American. After college, he played pro football briefly for the Calgary Stampeders of the Canadian Football League (CFL).

When his football career ended, Johnson began his career in wrestling in 1996 with the Tennessee-based United States Wrestling Association. He was a two-time USWA World Tag Team champion before signing with the WWF later that same year. In the WWF, he took the ring name Rocky Maivia and was heavily promoted as the WWF's first third generation wrestler. Despite his ring inexperience, he rapidly rose through the ranks. On February 13, 1997, he defeated Triple H for the Intercontinental Championship.

Maivia was a clean-cut babyface touted as the blue chipper. Fans began to resent his fast ascent. After losing the title, Rocky remerged as a heel and a member of the Nation of Domination led by Faarooq (Ron Simmons). Rocky began to insult the audience and other performers for booing his matches. To punctuate his heel

turn, he started referring to himself in third person as The Rock. He began a feud with Faarooq (Simmons) and eventually overthrew him to become leader of The Nation. As The Rock's popularity grew, infighting within the Nation reached a climax. In October 1998, he was defeated by Mark Henry with help from D'Lo Brown again turning babyface in the process.

The Rock was the second Black male to wear a recognized world heavyweight title in one of the major organizations and the first Black world champion in the WWF/E. He accomplished this feat on November 15, 1998 when he defeated Mankind (Mick Foley) for the WWF World Heavyweight Championship. He subsequently held that title on eight occasions. The Rock is also recognized as a two-time WCW world heavyweight champion. He won the title during The Invasion storyline against Booker T and avenging his title loss to Chris Jericho. After the Invasion storyline ended, the title was renamed the World Heavyweight Championship.

As his budding acting career grew, The Rock had more signature matches. The first was defeating Hulk Hogan in an Icon versus Icon match in 2002. The following year, also at Wrestlemania, he pinned Stone Cold Steve Austin in what was Austin's last match. As a charismatic performer, The Rock is known for raising his eyebrow and referring to himself as "The People's Champion." His signature moves are the Rock Bottom and the People's elbow.

The Rock's immense talent was accompanied by his tremendous charisma and ability to connect with fans. His interviews and catchphrases added words to the American pop cultural lexicon and he parlayed that crossover appeal into a very successful career in film, television and music. In 2012, Johnson created Seven Buck Productions with his first wife producer and IFBB professional bodybuilder Dany Garcia. In 2019, he was named one of Time magazine's 100 most influential people in the world. The Rock's career is perhaps summed up best by one of his catchphrases: he is the most electrifying man in sports entertainment.

Although he spends more time making movies these days than wrestling, he still makes sporadic appearances in the ring, much to the delight of his millions (and millions) of fans.

BOOKER T

Robert Booker Tio Huffman, Jr. is one of the most illustrious African American professional wrestlers and arguably the most decorated wrestler of his era. He has held the top title in three major wrestling promotions and is among a handful of wrestlers recognized as both a Triple Crown champion and a Grand Slam champion (four major titles) in the two largest North American wrestling promotions – World Championship Wrestling (WCW) and WWE.

Booker T is a six-time world heavyweight champion. He won the WCW World Heavyweight Championship five times and the WWE world title once. He is the second Black world champion in WCW (after Ron Simmons) and the second Black world champion in WWE (after The Rock). He was the final world champion and United States heavyweight champion in WCW simultaneously. He was the first African American to win the world television championship in WCW – a title he held for a record six times. Booker also held the world tag team title 10 times in WCW with his older brother Stevie Ray as Harlem Heat. He was also a world tag team champion three times in the WWE partnering with Test, Rob van Dam and Goldust. After winning the WWE's King of the Ring in 2006, he began the

King Booker persona along with his wife Queen Sharmell. After leaving the WWE, Booker joined Total Nonstop Action. In TNA, he

held the world tag team title with Scott Steiner and was the inaugural TNA Legends Champion (now the television champion).

Booker T was the consummate in-ring performer due to his athletic background. In high school, he once was a drum major in the marching band. His signature scissors kick and spinaroonie moves were incorporated into wrestling from band and hip-hop break dancing. He may not have reached mainstream crossover appeal, but

Booker T and Stevie Ray holding the WCW world tag team titles.

he has remained at the top of the business since winning the WCW World Heavyweight Championship on July 9, 2000. He captured the vacated belt by pinning Jeff Jarrett. However, his dominance in the mid-1990's, came as one-half of the Harlem Heat (with his brother Stevie Ray), who held the WCW World Tag Team titles for a record 10 times.

Booker started in the business with Stevie Ray as the Huffman brothers in Ivan Putski's Western Wrestling Alliance. After the company folded, the brothers joined Dallas-based Global Wrestling Federation as the Ebony Experience. They won the GWF Tag Team championship in 1992. They held the tag team titles for a record three times. In August 1993, they joined World Championship Wrestling as Harlem Heat. Billed from Harlem, NY, Booker was renamed Kole and Lash was renamed Kane. In 1994, they were managed by "Sister" Sherri Martel and resumed using their ring names Booker T and Stevie Ray. In December, they won the World Tag Team Championship by defeating Stars and Stripes. Harlem Heat went on to have feuds with the best talent in WCW including Sting & Lex Luger, Rick & Scott Steiner, American Males, Public Enemy and the Outsiders - Scott Hall and Kevin Nash.

In July 1997, they fired Sherri and later hired Jacqueline as their new manager. Stevie Ray took a few months off to recover from an ankle injury. During this time, Jacqueline joined the WWF and Booker became a singles competitor winning his first World Television title. When Stevie Ray returned, he joined the nWo. Booker eventually convinced him to leave the group and they reformed Harlem Heat in 1999. The duo went on to win the tag team titles three more times. Later that year, female wrestler Midnight became Harlem Heat's new manager. Booker liked the addition of Midnight, but Stevie Ray did not. He eventually turned on both Booker and Midnight. Stevie briefly formed Harlem Heat 2000 with Big T (known as Ahmed Johnson in WWF). The gimmick was short lived after Booker and Billy Kidman defeated Harlem Heat 2000 at the Uncensored pay-per-view. In 2015, Harlem Heat reunited for one last match in Booker and Sharmell's Reality of Wrestling.

They won their final tag team championship from the New Heavenly Bodies. In 2019, Harlem Heat was inducted into the WWE Hall of Fame. As a singles competitor, Booker T became one of the few wrestling stars to win championships in different major wrestling federations. He held titles in WCW, WWF/WWF and TNA. Booker is now a commentator for the WWE as well as operating Reality of Wrestling.

Booker T was inducted into the WWE Hall of Fame as a singles competitor in 2013 by his brother Stevie Ray. In 2022, he inducted his wife Queen Sharmell into the WWE Hall of Fame.

JAZZ

Carlene Denise Moore-Begnaud, who wrestles under the name Jazz, is the first African American female wrestler to hold the world title in two different major wrestling organizations. Jazz came onto the national pro wrestling scene in 1999 with the original ECW promotion where she first appeared as a manager/valet and wrestler as a part of the Impact Players before the promotion went bankrupt.

She joined the World Wrestling Federation in 2001. She made an instant impact and by the following year was feuding with the WWF Women's Champion Trish Stratus. On February 4, 2002, she became the second Black female to win a recognized world championship when she defeated Stratus for the WWF women's world title. Later that year, the WWF changed its name to WWE. Jazz continued to feud with several top wrestlers and regained the title on April 27, 2003 by again defeating Stratus. She lost the title in a battle royal to Gail Kim due to injury. Jazz was released from WWE in 2004.

After spending time on the independent circuit, she eventually joined the National Wrestling Alliance. Jazz won the NWA world women's championship on September 16, 2016. Her historic run as champion lasted 948 days, which is the third longest reign in the NWA's history after Debbie Combs and the Fabulous Moolah.

After more than two decades in the business, The Female Fighting Phenom is officially retired from active wrestling. In addition to the NWA and WWF/WWE titles, she held several titles with independent wrestling promotions. Jazz also owns a wrestling school with husband/wrestler Rodney Mack.

RON KILLINGS

Ron Aaron Killings is a professional wrestler and rapper from Charlotte, North Carolina. He holds the distinction of being the only African American wrestler to hold the NWA World Heavyweight Championship. He won that title twice when the TNA promotion was still affiliated with the National Wrestling Alliance (NWA).

In high school, Killings excelled in football and track & field. He also developed a love for rap music and breakdancing.

Killings received several college scholarships but turned them down to focus on a career in music. To finance his music career, he began selling drugs. After spending 13 months in prison, Killings ended his involvement in the drug lifestyle. While in a halfway house, he met cameraman Jackie Crockett of the NWA. He eventually decided to become a wrestler and trained with Manny Fernandez for three years.

He signed a contract with the World Wrestling Federation in 1999 using the ring name K-Kwik. After a title reign as the Southern Heavyweight Champion in the WWF's Memphis territory, Killings was promoted to the main roster. He debuted as tag team partners with Road Dogg Jessie James. K-Kwik became a singles competitor after Road Dogg was released in 2001. He won the Hardcore Championship twice in two days due to the 24/7 rules.

Killings joined Total Nonstop Action wrestling in 2002. He began using his real name and wrestled as Ron "The Truth" Killings. He is best known for his accomplishments in TNA by winning the

NWA World Heavyweight Championship. Killings' first reign as NWA world champion began on August 7, 2002 when he defeated Ken Shamrock. He won it again a year later in a four-way title match against A.J. Styles, Raven and Chris Harris.

Killings' many ring names have included "K-Krush," "K-Kwik," and "R-Truth" as he has gone between the WWE and TNA promotions. Currently using the R-Truth moniker in WWE, he has been relegated mostly to mid-card status. In 2019, Mick Foley announced the new WWE 24/7 Championship. Pro wrestling is known for gimmick matches because many have been successful entertainment segments. Most recently Truth has been a major player in the battle for the 24/7 championship. His charisma and athleticism has given a degree of interest to a relatively meaningless title. R-Truth has won the title over 50 times and in June 2019 was voted the fan favorite 24/7 champion.

AWESOME KONG

Kia Michelle Stevens is an actor and retired professional wrestler from Carson, California. WWE women's legend Lita, provided inspiration for Stevens to become a wrestler. She was a former contestant on the reality television show *Discovery Healthy Body Challenge* in 2002. In her attempts to lose weight on the show, she was introduced to professional wrestling trainer Jesse Hernandez. Stevens later appeared on the WWE's reality show *Tough Enough 2* in pursuit of a contract with the company. She did not earn a spot with the company but was invited to further training with All Japan Women's Pro Wrestling. Debuting in Japan under the ring name Amazing Kong – as a replacement for Japanese wrestler Aja Kong - she quickly found success as a performer. In 2004, she won the WWWA World Singles Championship; which is the top singles title in All Japan Pro Wrestling. She later teamed with Aja Kong in Gaea wrestling promotion to win the AAAW Tag Team championship.

In 2007, Kong won the AWA Japan World Women's Championship. She also appeared on the American independent circuit along with her AWA championship. In May, she won the NWA World Women's title in a champion versus champion match. Thus becoming a joint champion. In October 2007, Stevens debuted on Total Nonstop Action (TNA) wrestling's flagship TV show *Impact!* where her name was changed to "Awesome Kong." She immediately rose to the top of the women's (referred to in TNA as "Knockouts") division by winning the TNA Women's Knockout Championship. She joined Jacqueline Moore and Jazz as only the third Black female to hold a women's world title in a recognized, major North American wrestling promotion.

In December 2010, Stevens signed with the WWE under the ring name Kharma. She made her debut in May 2011 attacking the WWE Divas Champion Michelle McCool. In her first and only official WWE match, she returned at the 2012 Royal Rumble as the 21st entrant. Stevens became the third female to participate in the men's Royal Rumble match.

Her last run was with All Elite Wrestling from 2019-2021. She collaborated with Brandi Rhodes to form the Nightmare Collective. The idea was poorly received by audiences and was dropped in 2020. Stevens took a break to film the television series GLOW for Netflix.

After not appearing on AEW for over a year, the company decided not to renew her contract in June 2021. She announced her retirement from professional wrestling in August 2021. In October 2021, Stevens was inducted into Impact Wrestling's Hall of Fame.

MARK HENRY

Mark Henry was a well-known weightlifter/powerlifter who competed in the 1992 Summer Olympic Games held in Barcelona, Spain and the 1996 Olympics in Atlanta, Georgia. He started his wrestling career with the WWE in 1996. After a short run with the Nation of Domination and later the "Sexual Chocolate" persona, he left the WWE for Ohio Valley Wrestling to hone his skills. He also competed in strongman contests and solidified the "World's Strongest Man" title he used in the ring after winning the inaugural Arnold (Schwarzenegger) Strongman Classic.

Henry returned to WWE and in 2003 he was a member of Teddy Long's "Thuggin and Buggin' faction. In 2006, he was involved in main event feuds with Goldberg, Triple H, the Undertaker and Booker T. On June 29, 2008, Henry won the ECW World Championship by beating The Big Show and Kane in a 3-way title match. While this was considered his first world championship, ECW was a brand owned by World Wrestling Entertainment (WWE) at the time of his title reign. It was at the Night of Champions in 2011 when Henry defeated Randy Orton to win the World Heavyweight Championship. He had several successful title defenses and continued to wrestle despite being plagued with injuries. In 2018, he was inducted into the WWE Hall of Fame.

In 2021, he joined the All Elite Wrestling (AEW) promotion where he currently is a commentator. Henry's transition from performer to commentator has had rapid success. As a commentator, he is known for the signature line, "It's time for the main event."

KOFI KINGSTON

Kofi Nahaje Sarkodie-Mensah was born in Ghana, West Africa. As a young man, his family moved to the United States. He graduated from Winchester High School in Massachusetts and later Boston College. He started wrestling in 2005 with organizations in the New England territories including the NWA, Chaotic Wrestling, Millennium Wrestling and New England Championship Wrestling. In 2006, he signed with the WWE and was billed as a Jamaican wrestler using the name Kofi Kingston.

Kingston worked his way through the developmental ranks in Deep South Wrestling and Ohio Valley Wrestling before joining Florida Championship Wrestling (now NXT). After competing in NXT and ECW, Kingston was drafted to the *Raw* brand in 2008. In his first match, he defeated Chris Jericho for the Intercontinental Championship. After losing the title, he began a partnership with then WWE champion CM Punk. The duo eventually won the World Tag Team titles. After losing the titles, Kingston returned to singles wrestling. In 2009, he defeated Montel Vontavious Porter (MVP) for the United States Championship.

In April 2019, Kinston reached another milestone by defeating Daniel Bryan at Wrestlemania to win the WWE World Heavyweight Championship. With the win, Kingston became the first African-born Black world heavyweight champion. Kingston is a Triple Crown and Grand Slam champion in WWE. Throughout his career, he has won the Intercontinental title four times, the United States championship three times and he is a 14-time tag team champion in addition to his reign as world heavyweight champion. His other accolades include being named *Pro Wrestling Illustrated's* Tag Team of the Year (2012, with R. Truth), Tag Team of the Year (2015 & 2016, with The New Day) and Best Gimmick by the Wrestling Observer Newsletter. Kingston continues to compete in singles competition and tag team with The New Day.

BOBBY LASHLEY

Franklin Roberto Lashley, known professionally as Bobby Lashley, is a champion amateur wrestler, professional wrestler and mixed martial artist. "The Almighty" Bobby Lashley is the fifth Black male to win the world title in the WWE and by some accounts, the first to win the title in three different promotions. He is an eight-time world title holder. Lashley is a four-time Impact Wrestling champion, two-time WWE champion and two-time ECW champion. However, ECW was a brand owned by the WWE at the time he won the title.

The Kansas native, who is also Panamanian, was introduced to wrestling in junior high school primarily to train during football's offseason. He was a National Association of Intercollegiate Athletics (NAIA) national wrestling champion while a student at Missouri Valley College. Already an accomplished amateur wrestler, he continued to compete while serving in the U.S. Army. He exploded onto the professional wrestling scene in 2005 in the WWE. By the time Lashley appeared in ECW, it was not the original independent promotion, but the brand now owned by the WWE. On December 3, 2006, he defeated The Big Show, Test, CM Punk, Rob van Dam and Hardcore Holly in a 6-man elimination match to win the ECW World Heavyweight Championship. Lashley is the first Black wrestler to hold that version of the title and he had two reigns as ECW champion.

On March 19, 2007, Lashley became the only person to break the Masterlock hold – a swinging full nelson created by Chris Masters. This move later became one of Lashley's finishing moves, the hurt lock. He later moved into mixed martial arts (MMA) competitions and simultaneously returned to the wrestling ranks through the independent circuit and with the TNA promotion. On June 19, 2014, Lashley defeated Eric Young on an episode of Impact Wrestling to become the first African American to win the TNA World Heavyweight Championship. Throughout his tenure with the company, Lashley won the title four times.

Lashley eventually returned to the WWE. After joining forces with MVP and creating the Hurt Business, Lashley turned heel and won the WWE World Heavyweight title in March 2021 when he defeated The Miz on Raw. A few months later, Lashley lost the title to Big E. Lashley is a Grand Slam champion in WWE. He has held the following titles twice: WWE World Title, ECW World title, WWE Intercontinental title and the WWE United States Championship.

BIG E

Big E is the sixth Black male to hold the WWE's world heavyweight championship title. He has the distinction of being the first Black wrestler to win the WWE's Money in the Bank ladder match – which afforded him the opportunity to challenge for the title. Big E is also considered a Triple Crown champion in the WWE.

Ettore Ewen started wrestling in high school where he won a state championship. He later went to the University of Iowa where he played football. After an injury ended his football career, he made his wrestling debut as Big E Langston in Florida Championship Wrestling (FCW) in 2009. After WWE rebranded FCW as NXT, Langston went on to win the NXT Championship in 2013 by defeating Seth Rollins. He defeated Curtis Axel on November 18, 2013 to win the Intercontinental Championship, which was his first major championship. Big E teamed with Kofi Kingston and manager/wrestler Xavier Woods to form The New Day. They debuted in November 2014.

After winning both the Raw and Smackdown tag team titles, Big E returned to singles action. He won the Intercontinental title for the second time in 2020. He lost the title to Apollo Crews at Wrestlemania. Big E went on to win the Money in the Bank ladder match. On September 13, 2021, Big E used strategic timing to cash in his guaranteed world title match to challenge and defeat Bobby Lashley immediately after Lashley's grueling match against Randy Orton to win the WWE title. He is also the second member of the fan favorite trio The New Day to become world champion. After losing the title, he returned to tag team action with The New Day. In addition to winning the WWE title, he is known for winning the tag team titles eight times and the Intercontinental title twice. Big E is currently still active as a singles and tag team wrestler.

NYLA ROSE

Nyla Rose is a wrestler and actor of both African American and Native American heritage. She is the first Black Women's World Champion in All Elite Wrestling (AEW) and the first transgender woman to win a world title in a major wrestling company. Rose began her career in 2013 on the independent circuit mostly performing with the New Jersey-based Women Superstars Uncensored. Rose performed under the moniker "Native Beast," which was an ode to her Oneida heritage. She also wrestled with Japanese independent promotions before signing with AWE in 2019.

Rose debuted in the promotion's inaugural pay-per-view show Double or Nothing. She lost the fatal four-way match but made a grand introduction by spearing legendary wrestler Awesome Kong into the ring steps. Rose established herself as a bona fide heel when she attacked both Yuka Sakazaki and women's champion Riho after losing a triple threat match. Rose eventually defeated Riho on February 12, 2020, to win the women's title. She lost the title in May 2020 but remains in contention for another title shot.

XAVIER

John Jairo Bedoya, Jr. was the first Black world heavyweight champion in the Ring of Honor wrestling company. Bedoya's title reign was largely overlooked because Ring of Honor (ROH) was an upstart independent promotion at the time he won the title in 2002. However, the company has endured the test of time and ensuring that wrestling champions like Bedoya can get their due respect.

Bedoya debuted in 1995 on the independent circuit in New York City where he took the ring name Xavier. He wrestled in the first ROH show on February 23, 2002 defeating Scoot Andrews. He became the second champion in ROH history on September 21, 2002 with the victory over Low Ki. He successfully defended the title several times before losing to Samoa Joe in March 2003.

He made appearances in the World Wrestling Federation (WWF) in January 2002 and continued to make brief appearances in the WWE until 2007. He returned to ROH in a losing effort for the world championship against Bryan Danielson in 2006. Xavier also competed in mixed martial arts under the name John Xavier. He won his first fight in 14 seconds but lost his second fight by decision. Both fights were at the amateur ranks. In March 2020, Xavier was scheduled to face Jay Lethal in Ring of Honor's Past vs. Present event but the matches were cancelled due to the COVID-19 pandemic. He was known for his signature moves "Kiss Your X Goodbye" and "X 450." Bedoya died on August 16, 2020 at age 42.

JAY LETHAL

Jamar Shipman, who wrestles under the name Jay Lethal, is a two-time Ring of Honor (ROH) World Champion. He is a decorated Black American wrestler who currently has held 13 championships. Shipman started his career at age 16 in 2001 with Jersey All Pro Wrestling (JAPW). In JAPW, he won the television championship, and light heavyweight championship before becoming the heavyweight champion.

Shipman debuted in Ring of Honor (ROH) in 2003 as a member of Special K using the name Hydro. The following year, he left Special K and resumed using the name Jay Lethal. In March 2005, Lethal won the Pure Championship. He left the promotion in December to join Total Nonstop Action (TNA) Wrestling. After a few matches, Lethal participated in the Paparazzi Championship Series. In February 2007, TNA's *Impact!* Program ran a segment called "Paparazzi Idol." At the suggestion of Kevin Nash, who served as a judge, Lethal did a spot-on impression of Randy "Macho Man" Savage and began using the Black Machismo gimmick. In 2009, he won the X Division Championship. Lethal went on to win the TNA World Tag Team Championship with partner Consequences Creed (Xavier Woods).

After a brief hiatus from television, Lethal returned to *Impact!* In March 2010 with another successful legends imitation. This time, he mimicked Nature Boy Ric Flair, which led to a feud with Flair's group Fortune. Lethal went on to defeat Fortune member and X Division Champion Douglas Williams for his fourth title reign.

Lethal returned to Ring of Honor (ROH) in 2011. He won the World Television Championship two times before eventually capturing the World Heavyweight title in 2015. Lethal is the second

Black wrestler to hold the ROH World title and the longest reigning television champion. He is also a ROH Grand Slam Champion having held the World Heavyweight Championship twice, World Television Championship twice, Pure championship and the World Tag Team Championship with Jonathan Gresham, also a world heavyweight title holder.

JONATHAN GRESHAM

Jonathan Gresham is the third Black world heavyweight champion and a Triple Crown champion in Ring of Honor (ROH) wrestling. A native of Atlanta, Georgia, Gresham's career started in 2006 as Jonathan Davis. He performed for different promotions on the independent circuit including Booker T's Reality of Wrestling initially as Hero Tiger. He later reverted to his name Jonathan Gresham in 2014.

After continuing to wrestle for different promotions, Gresham signed with ROH in 2017. In 2019, Gresham teamed with Jay Lethal to win the ROH World Tag Team Championship by defeating the Briscoe Brothers. In 2020, Greshman emerged victorious from a 16-man tournament to win the Pure Championship. After losing the Pure Championship, Greshman went on to win the vacant ROH World Heavyweight Championship in December 2021 at the Final Battle pay-per-view. He won the title by defeating his former partner Jay Lethal. In March 2022, Greshman also won the Progress Wrestling World Championship from the British wrestling promotion.

Julian L.D. Shabazz & David L. Shabazz

SPECIAL MENTIONS: CHAMPIONS WITH AN ASTERISK

SPECIAL MENTIONS

We would be remiss if we did not highlight the Black champions who won the top titles but they were not recognized as true world titles. "Sailor" Art Thomas and Ernie Ladd both won a version of the WWA heavyweight title. However, since the organization was divided, the Indianapolis based group was not respected at the level of the faction where Bearcat Wright and Bobo Brazil competed. In spite of this, Thomas and Ladd deserve recognition for their accomplishments during a time when opportunity was scarce and nearly non-existent for Black professional wrestlers. Their sacrifice helped pave the way for the major promotions to eventually see that Black performers could draw crowds.

Ezekiel Jackson is another wrestling champion worthy of recognition, although he became champion after Extreme Championship Wrestling was no longer an independent promotion. Regardless, he is considered ECW's final world heavyweight champion and thus worthy of inclusion.

Another recent champion is Nelson Frazier, Jr. - the 6'9", 487-pound colossus known as Big Daddy V (Viscera). Big Daddy V was a world heavyweight champion in the short-lived Xcitement Wrestling Federation (XWF). The federation operated from 2001 -2002. The promotion attracted major stars including Hulk Hogan, Curt Hening, The Nasty Boys, Jimmy Hart, Jerry Lawler and others who were former stars in WWF/E, WCW and ECW. Frazier was the last champion in the XWF.

SAILOR ART THOMAS

Arthur Thomas was a Navy veteran of World War II and bodybuilder before entering the world of professional wrestling. On February 4, 1972, "Sailor" Arthur Thomas defeated Baron von Raschke in Detroit for the World Wrestling Alliance's (WWA) World Heavyweight crown. Unfortunately, the title was based in Indianapolis and not officially recognized by the organization. There was a dual world title situation in the WWA until, of course, the unification bout occurred between the two. Raschke won the match. Thomas, was originally used as a "plant" among the crowd. When the babyface (good guy) was being overpowered, he would emerge from the crowd and save the "face" from the heels or bad guys. Eventually, he became a wrestler and was one of the top Black performers in the business at the time.

Thomas worked another job while wrestling and could not be available to defend the title on a regular basis. His career as a bodybuilder and pro wrestler lasted over thirty years, as he was popular all across the globe. In 2016, he was inducted into the legacy wing of the WWE's Hall of Fame. Arthur Thomas died on March 20, 2002. He was 79.

ERNIE LADD

Ernest Ladd was a one-of-a-kind athlete who took his natural gifts to the highest level through wit and grit. He was a gifted two-sport athlete who excelled in basketball and football while growing up in Louisiana. Ladd went to Grambling State University on a basketball scholarship. He played basketball and football in college. In 1961, Ladd was drafted by the National Football League's (NFL) Chicago Bears and the American Football League's (AFL) San Diego Chargers. He decided to sign with the Chargers and won the AFL's championship in 1963. Ladd later played for the Houston Oilers and the Kansas City Chiefs. He was an AFL All-Star from 1962-65.

Ladd started wrestling in 1961 – the same year he was drafted to play professional football. He would compete part time during football's off-season. He began wrestling full-time in 1969. At 6'9" and weighing 290 pounds, Ladd was an imposing figure. He was the first Black character to successfully portray a "heel" or bad guy. During the 1970s, he was known in some territories as "The King" and "The Big Cat" in others. Ladd won the WWA heavyweight championship after defeating Dick the Bruiser in 1980. His title run was short but memorable. He lost the belt back after a month in a rematch.

Ladd's charisma allowed him to verbally joust at the same level as his physical skill. He would routinely insult his competitors calling them names like "pork chop belly" and referring to the programs hosts not by name but as "Mr. TV announcer" only. During the later years, he served as a manager for Afa and Sika, better known as the legendary tag team The Wild Samoans. Ladd retired from wrestling in 1986.

His athletic prowess has been duly noted. He was inducted into the San Diego Chargers Hall of Fame in 1981. In pro wrestling, he is among a handful of wrestlers to be inducted in both the WCW Hall of Fame (1994) and the WWE Hall of Fame (1995). Ernie Ladd died in 2007 at age 68.

EZEKIEL JACKSON

Rycklon Ezekiel Stephens is a retired wrestler and bodybuilder from Guyana. Stephens became a household name when he wrestled in the WWE under the name Ezekiel Jackson. Stephens started his career in 2007 with Ultimate Pro Wrestling as Big Ryck Hytz. Later that year, he signed with the WWE's Florida Championship Wrestling (now NXT) first using the name Rycklon. After a promotion to the main roster in 2008, the company changed his name to Ezekiel Jackson.

He first appeared in WWE as the bodyguard for Brian Kendrick and later wrestled in tag matches with Kendrick. In 2009, Jackson was drafted to the ECW brand. After a few months with ECW, Jackson found himself in a feud involving then-ECW champion Christian. In 2010, he faced Christian at the Royal Rumble in a losing effort. However, on February 16 – the last episode of ECW – Jackson defeated Christian for the world title in an Extreme Rules match. In 2014, Jackson made his TNA debut using the name Rycklon again. After a brief stint with TNA and the Lucha Underground, Jackson retired from professional wrestling in 2015.

BIG DADDY V

Nelson Frazier, Jr. was the first Black and final World Heavyweight Champion in the short-lived Xcitement Wrestling Federation (XWF). He is primarily known for his time in the WWF/WWE where he was a world tag team champion, hardcore champion and King of the Ring. Frazier used several ring names including Mabel, King Mabel, Viscera and Big Daddy V.

Frazier, a native of Goldsboro, NC, made his professional wrestling debut using the ring name Nelson Knight. He was a member of the tag team "The Harlem Knights" along with his storyline brother Bobby. They wrestled in the United States Wrestling Association, and won the Pro Wrestling Federation's tag team championship

twice before joining the World Wrestling Federation (WWF) in 1993. The duo was renamed Men on a Mission and Frazier renamed Mabel while "Bobby" (Robert Horne) became Mo. When Mabel turned heel, he received a push and won the 1995 King of the Ring tournament. After the victory, he was known as King Mabel and his tag team partner became Sir Mo. Mabel is the only wrestler in history awarded a King of the Ring championship belt. The best was never seen on WWF television. If the WWF officially adopted and recognized the belt, he would have been a Triple Crown champion.

Mabel was inexplicitly downgraded to mid-card status allegedly for his reckless style. As a superheavyweight, he weighed over 500 pounds. His signature move, the sitdown splash, injured several wrestlers. Mabel briefly wrestled on the independent circuit before returning to the WWF. In 1999, he joined the Undertaker's Ministry of Darkness as the enforcer Viscera. When the Ministry disbanded, he joined the hardcore division and won the hardcore championship.

Upon being released from his contract, he returned to the Memphis Wrestling promotion (formerly USWA) and even lost a boxing match to Rocky Johnson in 2003. He also made a brief appearance in Total Nonstop Action (TNA) in 2003 under his original ring name Nelson Knight. Then, he returned again to the WWE in 2004 as Viscera before transforming into the World's Largest Love Machine. He was paired with Trish Stratus, and became smitten with ring announcer Lilian Garcia and *Raw* bikini contest winner Candice Michelle. In 2007, he was drafted to the ECW brand and renamed Big Daddy V.

After leaving the WWE for the final time, he wrestled in the National Wrestling Alliance (NWA) and All Japan Pro Wrestling until 2011. His final match as Big Daddy V was in 2013 with Qatar Pro Wrestling. Frazier died of a heart attack on February 18, 2014.

CONCLUSION

Of the twenty-one past and current professional wrestlers profiled, 12 appeared in the original 2009 publication. A 75% increase over the last 13 years shows Black wrestlers have made progress. There are several current Black professional wrestlers with promise especially among the women wrestlers. In the WWE, Bianca Belair and Sasha Banks were the first Black women to headline the major pay-per-view Wrestlemania 37. Sasha also made history in 2022 with Naomi Fatu by becoming the first Black women's tag team champions in the WWE. In AEW, Nyla Rose is still a top contender for another reign as world champion. Additionally, newcomer and current television (TBS) champion Jade Cargill is dominating the competition with an undefeated winning streak reminiscent of Bill Goldberg.

Wrestling's popularity has increased again. While World Wrestling Entertainment (WWE) is still the dominant wrestling company with three brands spread across national television, All Elite Wrestling (AEW) is fast becoming a rival with national shows on two networks. With the financial backing of AEW, Ring of Honor (ROH) will become a major brand as well. Also, the former dominant National Wrestling Alliance (NWA and Impact Wrestling are still rebuilding in hopes of returning to major federation status. Based on wrestling's renewed popularity, there are many opportunities for Black wrestlers to display their talent.

AUTHOR'S NOTE

A book of such magnitude will undoubtedly include some unintentional errors, omissions, etc. The authors would appreciate, for the purpose of keeping future editions as accurate and complete as possible, if readers will send all corrections and/or additions to:

Awesome Records

P.O. Box 5523

Frankfort, KY 40601

ABOUT THE AUTHORS

Julian L. D. Shabazz *authored eight African-American themed books. He was a renowned public speaker, writer, scholar, college professor, historian, librarian and guest on television and radio.*

David L. Shabazz *is an accomplished writer and college professor. He is the author of Public Enemy Number One, Discover Your Gold Mind and Dolemite: The Story of Rudy Ray Moore.*

www.ingramcontent.com/pod-product-compliance
Lightning Source LLC
Chambersburg PA
CBHW020034120526
44588CB00030B/391